SPACE

EXTREME FACTS

BY STEFFI CAVELL-CLARKE

THE SECRET BOOK COMPANY

©This edition was published in 2018. First published in 2017.

The Secret Book Company
King's Lynn
Norfolk
PE30 4LS

ISBN: 978-1-912171-18-7

Written by:
Steffi Cavell-Clarke
Edited by:
Holly Duhig
Designed by:
Danielle Rippengill

All rights reserved
Printed in Malaysia

A catalogue record for this book is available from the British Library.

PHOTO CREDITS

CONTENTS

Page 4   Space
Page 6   Galaxies
Page 8   The Milky Way
Page 10   The Solar System
Page 12   Stars
Page 14   Planets
Page 16   The Sun
Page 18   The Moon
Page 20   Planet Earth
Page 22   Space Travel
Page 24   Glossary and Index

Words that look like <u>this</u> can be found in the glossary on page 24.

SPACE

Have you ever looked up at the stars and wondered just how big the universe is?

There are many mysterious things about space that not even scientists can answer, but there are some things that we DO know …

You wouldn't be able to survive in outer space because there isn't any air to breathe.

Don't think that you would be able to hold your breath either! If you held your breath in space, your lungs would explode and kill you instantly.

There is only a small amount of <u>gravity</u> in space, which means that you would float around in your space suit forever!

The universe is made up of all of time and space.

Many people believe that the universe began with a huge explosion called the Big Bang.

No one knows how exactly how many stars, planets and asteroids the universe holds.

The universe is constantly expanding, which means that it is always getting bigger.

The universe is about **13.8 billion years old,** but no one knows exactly how old it is.

GALAXIES

Galaxies are massive collections of stars that are held together by gravity.

There are three main types of galaxy.

Spiral Galaxy

Irregular Galaxy

Elliptical Galaxy

There are more than **170 billion** galaxies in the **universe.**

Some galaxies only contain about 10 million stars, but others contain over 100 trillion stars.

Galaxies are often very colourful and different galaxies can be different colours.

Astronomers believe that black holes lie in the centre of large galaxies.

A black hole is a point in space with such strong gravity that not even light can escape.

THE MILKY WAY

The galaxy that we live in is called the Milky Way.

The Milky Way is a spiral galaxy.

It has a black hole in the centre called Sagittarius A*.

The Milky Way began forming around 13 billion years ago.

There are up to 400 billion stars in the Milky Way.

The Milky Way is moving through space faster than **552 kilometres** per second. That's fast!

Planet Earth is located **26,000 light-years** away from the centre **of the Milky Way.**

We call our galaxy the Milky Way because, when looking at it from Earth, it looks like milk has been spilt across the sky.

THE SOLAR SYSTEM

The Sun is at the centre of the Solar System and the planets move around it in their <u>orbits</u>.

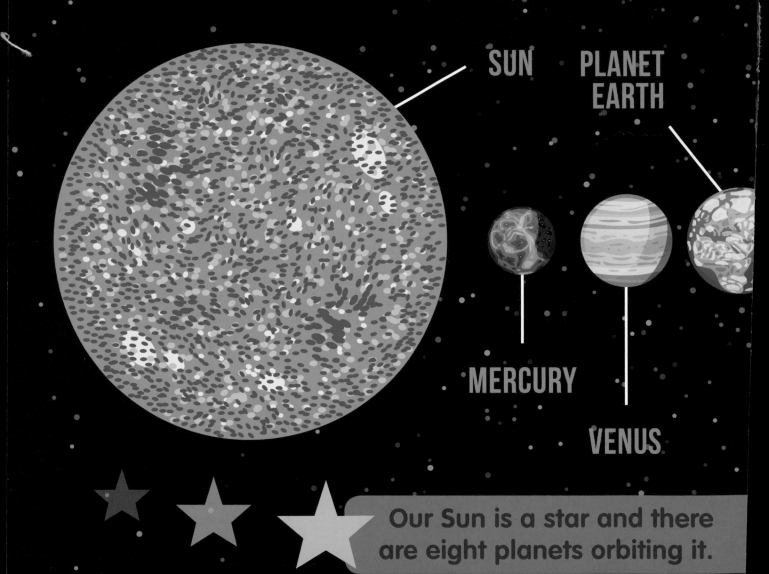

SUN

PLANET EARTH

MERCURY

VENUS

Our Sun is a star and there are eight planets orbiting it.

Everything in the Solar System orbits the Sun.

Asteroids are pieces of rock and metal that are too small to be called planets.

The Asteroid Belt is a band of asteroids that sits between Mars and Jupiter.

MARS

JUPITER

SATURN

URANUS

NEPTUNE

There are also moons, comets, dust and gases travelling around our Solar System.

STARS

A star is a huge ball of gas that <u>generates</u> light and energy. You can see stars in the night sky.

The average star lives for about **10 billion years.**

There are more stars in the universe than grains of sand on all the beaches on Earth. **That's at least one billion trillion stars.**

Our Sun is a star and it heats and lights planet Earth.

Stars seem to twinkle in the night sky, but this is just an illusion! The star's light gets disrupted as it passes though the Earth's atmosphere. This is what makes it look like it's twinkling.

Atmosphere

The Sun is actually a small star. Most other stars are bigger than the Sun.

The Sun only looks large because it is **close to Earth**.

One of the largest stars that we know about is called VY Canis Majoris. This star is around 2,000 times bigger than our Sun!

2,000 X   = VY Canis Majoris

PLANETS

A planet is a large object that orbits a star. Here are some fun facts about the planets in our Solar System.

A single day on Mercury lasts 176 days on Earth.

Planet Earth is the only planet in the Solar System that has life… as far as we know!

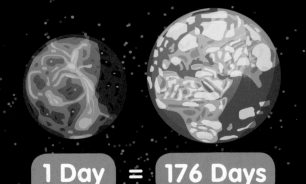

1 Day = 176 Days

The sunset on Mars is blue.

Venus

is the hottest planet in our Solar System. It has a surface temperature of **over 450 °C.**

You wouldn't be able to walk on **Jupiter, Saturn, Uranus** or **Neptune** because they have no **solid surface.**

Saturn has rings that are made of chunks of ice and rock.

Uranus is so far away from Earth that it would take about 9 years to get there in a spacecraft.

THE SUN

The Sun is so large that 1,300,000 Earths could fit inside it.

X 1,300,000 =

The Sun's light takes **8 minutes and 20 seconds** to travel from the Sun to the Earth.

The Sun is 4.6 **billion** years old.

As the Sun gets **older,** it gets hotter.

At its centre, the Sun reaches **temperatures of 15,000,000 °C!**

The Sun has a powerful **gravitational** pull that keeps the **planets** orbiting around it.

Without the Sun, there would be no life on Earth. Nearly every form of life on Earth needs sunlight to survive.

It is very dangerous to look directly at the Sun, even with sunglasses on!

Many ancient civilisations worshipped the Sun.

THE MOON

A moon is a natural object that orbits around a planet. Planet Earth has one moon, known as the Moon.

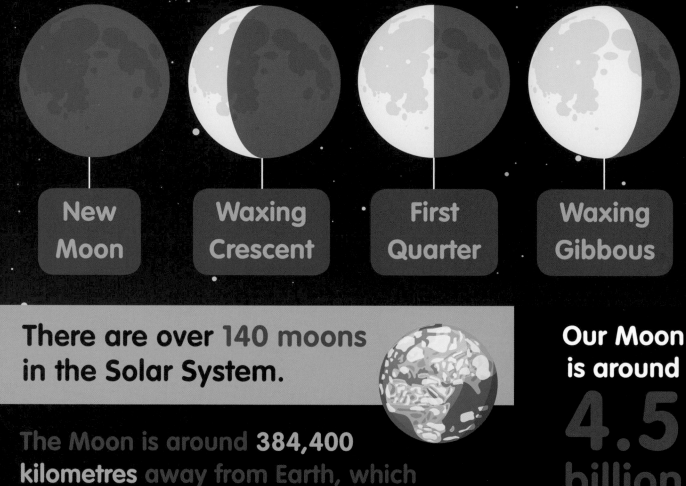

| New Moon | Waxing Crescent | First Quarter | Waxing Gibbous |

There are over 140 moons in the Solar System.

The Moon is around **384,400 kilometres** away from Earth, which makes it look a lot smaller than it is!

Our Moon is around 4.5 billion years old.

Even though the Moon is a sphere, it doesn't always look like that from Earth. This is because not all of it is illuminated all of the time.

Mankind has been to the Moon!

Footprints and tire tracks left on the Moon by <u>astronauts</u> will stay there forever as there is no wind to blow them away.

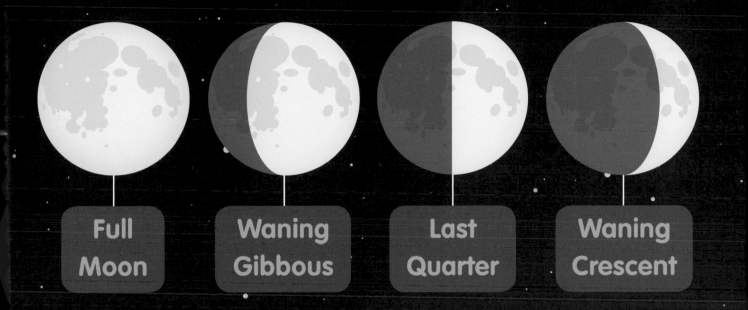

Full Moon

Waning Gibbous

Last Quarter

Waning Crescent

The first man on the Moon was Neil Armstrong. He first stepped on the Moon, using his left foot, on the 20th of July, 1969.

"One small step for [a] man, one giant leap for mankind"

There is very little gravity on the Moon, so astronauts who walk on the Moon wear heavy suits to weigh them down.

A space suit costs around $11 million!

19

PLANET EARTH

Home sweet home! Planet Earth is, in many ways, unlike any other planet in the Solar System.

It is the only planet that has <u>liquid</u> water on its surface.

It is the **only** planet in the Solar System that has life!

Did you know that people once believed the Earth was the centre of the universe?

Earth has an atmosphere that contains lots of <u>oxygen</u>, which humans and animals need in order to breathe.

Planet Earth is made of many layers.

Its inner core is made of a mixture of metals like iron and nickel.

Crust

Mantle

Outer Core

Inner Core

The core can reach temperatures of

6,000 °C!

SPACE TRAVEL

Space is so huge that it is measured in light years.

A light year is the distance that light would be able to travel in a year. One light year is about 9 trillion kilometres.

If we could travel at the speed of light, then we could explore a lot more of space!

Currently, spacecraft need 1.9 million litres of fuel just to get into space. After that, they can travel around 28,000 kilometres per hour.

Some people have said that space smells like metal. Others say it smells like raspberries!

Even though getting up into space can be challenging, it is important for human beings to know more about the universe that we live in and the history of the Earth.

In **1957**, a Russian dog called Laika was the first living thing to orbit the Earth.

Scientists are using technology to find new ways of exploring space. Robots have already been to Mars!

Humans have been looking for signs of life in space for centuries, but they haven't found anything yet! What do you think? Do you think that alien life is out there??

GLOSSARY

°C	the symbol for degrees Celsius, which is a measurement of temperature
astronaut	a person who is trained to travel in a spacecraft
astronomers	people who study the universe and objects in space
atmosphere	the mixture of gases that surround some planets in space, such as Earth
generates	makes
gravity	the force that attracts physical bodies together
liquid	something that flows, such as water
orbits	the paths that objects follow around larger objects in space
oxygen	a natural gas that all living things need in order to survive

INDEX

asteroids 5, 11

astronauts 19

black holes 7–8

galaxies 6–9

gravity 4, 6–7, 17, 19

light years 9, 22

moons 11, 18–19

Earth 9–10, 12–18, 20–21, 23

planets 5, 10–11, 14–15, 17–18, 20

Solar System 10–11, 14–15, 18, 20

spacecraft 15, 22

stars 4–8, 10, 12–14

Sun 10–13, 16–17

universe 4–5, 7, 12, 20, 23